37 Stress-Free Ways to Declutter Your Home

By Abigail Rosenberg

Table of Contents

Introduction

Are you sick of feeling stressed, overwhelmed, and as if you're drowning in *stuff?*

Do you long to make your home more streamlined and clean?

If you would like to declutter your home... and do it even if you feel completely overwhelmed and don't know where to begin... then this book will show you how.

If you've ever thought...

- "I've got too much stuff."

- **"I have tried to get organized but it just feels so**

overwhelming."

- "This clutter makes me so frustrated, sometimes to the point of almost freaking out."

- **"I feel like I can't calm down or find peace when my home is so full of clutter."**

- "Having a clean, organized, streamlined home gives me more energy and makes me feel lighter. *It almost feels like clutter is constantly draining me of energy.*"

- **"I find that not having the house in order is a constant daily stressor."**

- "I feel like I'm nearing a breaking point with all this clutter. I feel like I just can't handle it anymore. *I want it gone!*"

- **"I don't know where to begin."**

... then you're in the right place.

This book equips you with a surprisingly simple solution to an extraordinarily difficult problem.

As I'm sure you've found in your own life, there are two big obstacles to overcoming clutter:

1. **Getting started.** *Without* getting demotivated by the amount of clutter yet to tackle.

2. **Tackling clutter in a manageable, methodical manner.** You want decluttering to be relatively easy and stress-free, not overwhelming, stressful, and depressing.

So how do you overcome this (literal) mess?

How can you get started *without* getting overwhelmed and demotivated?

How do you tackle clutter in a way that is manageable,

methodical, and—dare I say—*fun*? (*Gasp*)

Well, my (currently) messy and distressed friend, fear not.

Inside these clean, crisp white pages, you'll find not one, not two, not even three, but 37 solutions to your messy situation.

Just *one* of these clutter-cleansing tips could transform your home from tornado-victim-lookalike to permanently ready for an open house.

Even better... use some of these strategies in conjunction with one another and you'll be astonished by the powerful clutter-banishing effect.

Something else you'll find is that even if you get bored with one method, you can try another. Heck, you can (if applicable) get the kids involved with some of the "decluttering challenges" you're about to discover (see: the "Making It Fun" section in *Part III* of this book).

For your convenience, this book has been broken down into four sections:

1. Getting Started
2. Cutting the Clutter
3. Making it Fun
4. Keeping Your Home Clutter-Free

Plus, at the end of the book, there is a bonus section on the Japanese KonMari decluttering method.

So let's dive right in cut the clutter!

PART I: GETTING STARTED

#1

Getting Started Tip #1: Start with a single small success.
Yes, I know, your house is an absolute mess. Every room, every cupboard, every draw, every table top. But that is *exactly* why you need to start with a small win. This is a big task that can feel overwhelming, and the only way you can get yourself through it is by breaking it down into smaller chunks. Start small—such as by putting 10 items back in their place. You'll feel much better than if you just try dive right in and attempt to conquer the entire house without the sense of accomplishment that comes from some "small wins" along the way. So go big, but start small. Narrow your vision from the entire house to that one small, solvable clutter problem. Just one counter, shelf, or drawer. That small success will motivate you and spur you onwards.

TAKE ACTION RIGHT NOW: Put this book down and go find *one* (no more, no less—just *one*) shelf/bench/drawer *right now* and declutter it. Put things where they belong, chuck out trash and unnecessary items, and perhaps donate a few items to your local charity. Get up and go do it!

#2

Getting Started Tip #2: Make an appointment with your clutter. No, not your doctor, but your clutter. You're busy. Your schedule is packed. But this damn clutter business is driving you nuts! So schedule an appointment and get to it, because it's not going to happen by itself (as much as you might wish it would).

TAKE ACTION RIGHT NOW: Put this book down, go grab your phone/diary/calendar (whatever you use to schedule things) and schedule a declutter session. Seriously, go do it right now! No excuses. It doesn't matter if it's 15 minutes or one hour, tomorrow morning or this weekend. Just go schedule a declutter session.

#3

Getting Started Tip #3: Fill one trash bag. This is a great technique—especially when you're just getting started—because there's a limit. You don't need to declutter the entire house. Just fill one trash bag of items to throw away (or donate). It's beautiful in it's simplicity.

TAKE ACTION RIGHT NOW: Get up, go grab a trash bag, and fill it up! For some extra spice, start a stopwatch and see how quickly you can do it. Once you're finished, chuck it in the trash (or, if they're items you can donate, in the boot of your car). Go!

#4

Getting Started Tip #4: Gather similar items together. Pencils, scissors, cereals, pants, and so on. Don't worry about whether or not you should chuck something out. Don't worry about where these categorized items should go. Just focus on grouping like items together.

TAKE ACTION NOW: Choose one category of items (e.g. toys or stationeries) and go group them all together in one place. Now!

#5

Getting Started Tip #5: Pick up five "homeless" items and find a home for them. Make sure that you actually use these items. Don't find a place for them if they belong in the trash can! Items that have no homes are always going to end up cluttering your house. So put an end to it by giving them a home—a specific place to put them when they're not in use. You can, of course, continue and do this for every lost item in your home, but start with just five. Heck, if you want, you could even make a habit of finding a home for five homeless items every day. In a few weeks, your house will be looking far better! Also note that you should make sure to alert the rest of the family about this belonging's new place so that they know where it goes when they're finished with it.

TAKE ACTION RIGHT NOW: Get up onto those feet of yours and go hunt for five homeless items! Go give them a home. Put a smile on that face of yours. After all, you're helping the homeless!

#6

Getting Started Tip #6: Empty a drawer. Sounds simple, doesn't it? *Exactly.* Just getting started is the most important thing. Once you've pulled everything out of that one (*only* one —don't get too ambitious just yet, start small) drawer, sort it into three piles: 1) stuff that should go in the trash; 2) stuff that belongs somewhere else; 3) stuff that really, *really* should actually be in that drawer. Put those things back in the draw (neatly and in an organized manner). Then chuck out and relocate the other two piles accordingly. Ta da! How's that feel? Great, eh? Bet you just can't wait to get started decluttering those other drawers.

TAKE ACTION RIGHT NOW: Go off *right now*, pick *one* messy drawer, and get to work! I don't want to see you again until you've done it!

#7

Getting Started Tip #7: Create a "starting zone" and get

to work clearing it. Your starting zone could be a couch (along with a four-foot perimeter around it), the kitchen table, or anything else. This is now officially a no-clutter zone. Anything that is not in use cannot be placed there—put it away instead! Once you've got your initial clutter-free zone up and running, steadily expand it every day until the entire house has been consumed.

TAKE ACTION RIGHT NOW: Go on! Off you go, go find an initial "clutter-free zone." Clear it of clutter. That's it. Nothing too big. Shouldn't take any longer than five minutes (10 at most). Now, every day from now, gradually expand that clutter-free zone. Now go off and get started!

#8

Getting Started Tip #8: Five minutes. That's all. Get up. Set a timer for five minutes on your phone. Declutter like mad until the timer buzzes. You can spend the five minutes chucking old stuff in the trash, putting things back where they belong, or organizing stuff that's got strewn all over the place. Simple. If you want, you can make this into a daily habit. It's quick (five minutes) yet rewarding. Maybe do it every morning before having a shower (and/or every evening before eating dinner).

TAKE ACTION RIGHT NOW: Put this book down, set a timer, and—until the timer buzzes—declutter like your life depends on it! I'm dead serious. Don't read on until you've done it. It takes five minutes for goodness' sake!

#9

Getting Started Tip #9: Make a list of places in your home, declutter them one at a time. Remarkably simple, highly effective.

TAKE ACTION RIGHT NOW: Put this book down and go grab a piece of scrap paper (or a notebook). Make a list of all the different areas in your home, beginning with the easiest area to declutter (which is probably a bathroom) down to the toughest (likely the kitchen, living area, or a bedroom). As soon as you've finished writing that list, go declutter the area at the top of your list (i.e. the easiest area). *However*, as soon as you've finished decluttering that one area, STOP! Work on the rest of the list later (or even schedule it!) Anyway, go! What are you still reading this for? Go get making that list, checking it twice, gonna find out where's cluttered and... *ahem* excuse me.

#10

Getting Started Tip #10: Kill the torturer. What in your cluttered home pains you the most? Is it tripping over in the garage on your way to the car each morning? Is it accidently knocking things off your bedside table when you get up to go to the toilet in the middle of the night? Is it not being able to find that cereal box every morning? Is it a home office so full of clutter that just drives you absolutely nuts? A wardrobe that seems to just consume clothes, never to be found again? Find that one thing that most annoys, frustrates, or overwhelms you. *One* thing. Start there. *Only* there. Don't start decluttering anywhere else until that torturous area has been subdued.

TAKE ACTION RIGHT NOW: Go subdue that torturous, monstrous, mountain of clutter right *now!* (Before it drives you so crazy someone has to sign you into a mental ward!) Go!

PART II: CUTTING THE CLUTTER

#1

Cutting the Clutter Tip #1: Use "The Four-Box Method".
The four boxes used in the four-boxed method are as follows:
1) stuff to throw away; 2) stuff to give away; 3) stuff to put away
(i.e. relocate); and 4) stuff to keep. Put simply, trash, donate,
relocate, and keep. You can mark those four boxes with the
respective names, if you so wish. As you set out on your
declutter crusade, take these four boxes with you. Drawer to
drawer. Cupboard to cupboard. Room to room. Chuck items in
one of the four boxes: trash, donate, relocate, or keep. Let no
item escape the wrath of these four boxes until your whole
house is rid of clutter.

TAKE ACTION RIGHT NOW: Go grab four boxes
(whether cardboard or plastic) or bags. Identify *one*
area/cupboard/drawer/bench/table. Take these four horsemen
along with ye and bring Armageddon to this damned clutter-
hell.

#2

Cutting the Clutter Tip #2: If you don't love it, don't keep it. In other words, as you go about bringing order to your humble but clutter-stricken abode, follow the aforementioned rule (if you don't love it, don't keep it). Sometimes we feel like we're obligated to keep something just because we spent our hard-earned cash on it. But really, if you never use it and it only contributes to your clutter-induced stress, it's better off in a landfill (or charity store). So chuck out everything you don't love or *absolutely need*.

TAKE ACTION RIGHT NOW: This is going to be really simple. So even if (much to my dismay) you've ignored a couple of the previous call to arms, I strongly urge you to not skip this quick exercise. Ready for it? Here it is: *Go find ONE item that you don't* love *and chuck it in the trash.* Ta da! That's it. Can't get much simpler than that. Now go!

#3

Cutting the Clutter Tip #3: Create a "maybe" box for six months from now. As ye go about combing through your almighty mountains of cursed mess, bring with ye a blessed little box upon which is inscribed the word "maybe". Whenever ye find yeself in the wrath of doubt, toss thy item into thy "maybe" box. Cutting the archaic language, it comes down to this: We largely know the items we need to keep and the items that can go in the trash. But every now and then we encounter an item we're not so certain about. Will I regret tossing it? Or will it just continue to needlessly clutter the house? Toss such items into the "maybe" box. Once you've finished decluttering, put this "maybe" box somewhere where it's out of the way (maybe on top of a cupboard in the garage, or in the attic or basement). Set yourself a reminder (or put it on your calendar) to go get that box in six months. If you haven't had to go take anything out of the box (i.e. to use it) for six months, you can safely toss them all in the trash.

TAKE ACTION NOW: Create a "maybe" box (or bag), schedule a decluttering session (whether for five minutes or 60 minutes, and toss any "maybe" items into the "maybe" box/bag.

#4

Cutting the Clutter Tip #4: Pack up to move. But don't actually move. Just pack everything up into boxes as if the moving truck was about to show up and move all your stuff across the country. Now, just leave those boxes there and keep on living life. If you need something, take it out, use it, and return it to it's original place. After three months (or, if you really want, six months) take a look at what's still in those boxes. Chuck them in the trash or give them away. You don't need them, you don't use them, and all they do is clutter up your house and cause you stress for absolutely no reason at all. Is this an extreme way to eliminate useless clutter? Yes. But is it effective? Hell yes!

TAKE ACTION RIGHT NOW: Because you almost certainly will not pack up your entire house just because I said so, I will give you a smaller challenge in this "Take Action Right Now" section. Here it is: Start with *one* room. Ideally the most cluttered and overwhelming room. Chuck *everything* (except big pieces of furniture, of course) into a few big boxes. Go put those clutter-filled boxes into the basement or garage. Whenever you need to use something from those boxes, go grab it, use it, and put it back in its original place (not the box). After three to six months, get rid of everything else that remains in the box(es).

#5

Cutting the Clutter Tip #5: Ensure that you only have one of everything. You don't need five different types of coffee, six different brands of cereal, and god-only-knows how many different pairs of shoes. Simplify, simplify, simplify! Choose your favorite type of coffee and get rid of the rest. Choose your favorite cereal and stick with it. Select only a *few* of your favorite shoes and donate the rest. Seriously. Think of the 80/20 rule. 20 percent of your "stuff" gets used 80 percent of the time, while the other 80 percent of "stuff" does little more than clutter up your home and stress you out. Toss the 80 percent of stuff that never gets used and keep the 20 percent of stuff you use all the time.

TAKE ACTION RIGHT NOW: Go find (and toss) *one* thing that you don't need because you already own several other ones. It might be that you have 20 highlighters or a dozen different "Happy Birthday" mugs. *Go!*

#6

Cutting the Clutter Tip #6: Create a "capsule wardrobe." Continuing the idea of applying the 80/20 rule to decluttering above, simplify your wardrobe. Apply the 80/20 rule to the clothes you wear. Come on, you know it's true. You might have three wardrobes full of clothes, but in reality, 20 percent of those clothes get worn 80 percent of the time while everything else hardly ever sees the light of day. While you don't need to go hardcore like Steve Jobs and Mark Zuckerberg and wear the same thing every day, you and I both know you can significantly simplify your wardrobe. Do you *really* need hundreds of different articles of clothing? Simplify, simplify, simplify! We've all walked up to our closet at one point or another and felt like we've had nothing to wear, despite the closet being completely full. That's a surefire sign that you're in desperate need of a declutter. Just pick your very favorite clothes and chuck out the rest. You could even order a few of the same pieces of clothing in different colors. Remember: 80 percent of your clothes get worn only 20 percent of the time, while 20 percent get worn 80 percent of the time. Try eliminate as many of those "80-percent" clothes as possible.

TAKE ACTION RIGHT NOW: Once again, this challenge is dead simple and shouldn't take you any longer than five to 10 minutes. Go find *one* item of clothing that you know you almost never wear and toss it or give it away.

#7

Cutting the Clutter Tip #7: Take the 33x3 challenge. What's the 33x3 challenge? Here it is: Wear only 33 articles of clothing for three months. And yes, that includes shoes. Seriously, you and I both know you don't need a hundred different piles of stuff that's been sold to you as the latest and greatest fashion trend. Narrow down to the 20 percent that you wear 80 percent of the time and eliminate the rest. Challenge yourself to live with less and learn from the experience. Remember: 33 for three months.

TAKE ACTION RIGHT NOW: Pull out a piece of scrap paper or a notebook and write down your favorite 33 articles of clothing—the ones you wear the most. That's it. Should take no longer than five minutes, so go do it!

#8

Cutting the Clutter Tip #7: Store things near where you use them. This tip seems almost stupidly obvious, but you'd be surprised by how much it indirectly contributes to clutter. When it's an inconvenience to put something away (even if only a very minor one), it becomes all too easy to just leave things lying around as clutter.

TAKE ACTION RIGHT NOW: Go find one item that always seems to end up lost lying around somewhere amongst the clutter. Now that you have it, store it in a place right next to where you use it. So if you have a hand-held blender that you use every morning but always seems to end up lying around the place, go put it in the draw *directly* below where you use it. Make it as easy as possible for yourself. Conversely, if you have a turkey-roasting pan that you only ever use once a year, make sure it's not taking up prime real estate in the kitchen.

#9

Cutting the Clutter Tip #9: Follow the rule of five. Every time you clean a room, get rid of five things you don't use. Chuck them in the trash, donate them, or sell them on eBay.

TAKE ACTION RIGHT NOW: Okay, not *right now*, but next time you clean a room—whether it be tidying up the toys strewn across the floor in one of the kid's bedrooms or cleaning your bathroom—toss out (or donate/sell) five items. It could be some old toys that the kids no longer play with. Or some empty bottles in your bathroom. Five things. That's it.

#10

Cutting the Clutter Tip #10: Thou shalt label thy shelves. Labeling shelves (and other areas, if necessary) saves time that would otherwise be spent looking for things. It also ensures everything has a place—canned goods, cereals, pasta, and so on. You can also label the drawers in your office—and other spaces —accordingly. If you have kids, you could label the shelves in their bedroom with pictures to help them keep their toys organized.

TAKE ACTION RIGHT NOW: Get up out of ye chair and go find one drawer or shelf. Determine what it is that should go there (even if you pantry/drawer/etc. currently looks not dissimilar to a warzone). Then, go cut a small piece of paper (slightly less than the width of a piece of sticky tape), write down the specific type of item that will now inhabit this area (e.g. canned goods, stationeries, kids lunchboxes, stuffed teddy bears, whatever) and stick your new label there. From now on, nothing else is to be allowed in this [insert item type] sanctuary. And, if any items not currently in use escape this sanctuary, they must be hunted down and returned to the refuge.

#11

Cutting the Clutter Tip #11: Thou shalt make the most of 21st century technology. Put simply, "outsource" your clutter. A decade or two ago, we needed *sooo* many different things. A radio, VCR player, camera, camcorder, TV, telephone, books, encyclopedias, gaming consoles, and so on. Now, all of that has merged into a single device: Your smartphone. So that begs the question: Why have hundreds of DVDs (or, god help you, VCR tapes) when you have Netflix? (Or, you cheeky bugger, Pirate Bay-like torrent sites?) Similarly, why have countless magazines when you can access them all at your local public library? Why do you need all those dust-collecting recipe books when you can look them up online? (Or get them on your kindle?) You can also scan and upload pictures and important documents to a computer hard drive or cloud storage service such as Google Drive or DropBox. If you're super keen, see if you can set something up with your neighbour where you share/swap garden tools and/or hobby equipment. The options are limitless!

TAKE ACTION RIGHT NOW: Go find *one* thing you can "outsource." A document you can scan and upload to Google Drive. A DVD you can watch on Netflix. Just *one* thing. Go!

#12

Cutting the Clutter Tip #12: Use the "what would I save from a fire?" rule. It's easy to get caught up in the joy of decluttering and start seeing everything as just "stuff". But hold back from going *too* overboard by asking yourself, "What would I save from a fire?" It might be some photographs, or something else important. Asking yourself this question will help prevent you from throwing something out on a whim that you'll later come to regret. So get rid of as much as possible, but don't make the mistake of chucking out the things that are particularly important. You know, the kind of things that you'd like to share with your grandchildren someday.

#13

Cutting the Clutter Tip #13: When in doubt, ask yourself if you would buy it. It's a remarkably simple yet highly effective way at approaching decluttering. Ask yourself, "If I was just buying this now, how much would I pay?" This should help overcome some difficulties you might encounter when removing unneeded clutter.

TAKE ACTION RIGHT NOW: Go find one item you've been humming and harring over and ask yourself, "If I was just buying this now, how much (if anything) would I pay for it?"

PART III: MAKING IT FUN

#1

Making It Fun Tip #1: Take the 12-12-12 challenge. The 12-12-12 challenge is a fun way to get started decluttering. Locate 12 items to toss, 12 to donate, and 12 to be put back in their proper place. If you have a significant other and/or kids, you can get them involved and see who can complete the 12-12-12 challenge the quickest.

TAKE ACTION RIGHT NOW: Get up and go! Find 12 things you can chuck in the bin, 12 to donate, and 12 to be returned to their proper home. Go, go, go!

#2

Making It Fun Tip #2: Give something away every day. You'll be reducing your stuff one day at a time—easy.

TAKE ACTION NOW: Go find one item *right now* to give away or donate.

#3

Making It Fun Tip #3: The penicillin method.
Decluttering efforts often find themselves quickly reversed as
the clutter ebbs and flows. You get into a decluttering frenzy
and declutter an entire room, but a week later, the clutter is
back. Fortunately, there's a solution: The penicillin method.
The penicillin method works like a researcher applying drops
of penicillin (thus the methods namesake) to a petri dish of
mold spores. Each drop rids the area of the unwanted intruder,
until eventually, the entire dish is clear. Apply this metaphor to
your decluttering methods by clearing a single spot—say the
kitchen table—by inoculating it with imaginary penicillin. That
is, never allowing clutter to return to that disinfected area. Do a
daily clutter check if need be. Then, apply some penicillin to
another area. And another. Eventually, these clutter-inoculated
areas will link up and before you know it, your entire home is a
clutter-free zone. Why is the penicillin method so effective?
Apart from engaging your imagination and making decluttering
a bit more fun, it focuses you on *prevention* (i.e. not allowing
any clutter in the penicillin-infused areas).

TAKE ACTION RIGHT NOW: Find one small area and inject it with penicillin. Right now! Go!

#4

Making It Fun Tip #4: Establish clutter preserves. We all know about forest and wildlife preserves, but it's not just legislative bureaucrats that get to have all the fun creating preserves. You too can create a preserve—a clutter preserve! As much as we may wish it were not the case, clutter is a part of living (unless you go become a monk, that is). But you can still make the most of this (and even have fun with it!) by establishing a few dedicated clutter preserves. In the limited boundaries of these clutter preserves, like wildlife preserves, clutter can live freely. For example, a chair could become your bedroom's clutter preserve, home to the occasional tossed item of clothing. Your kitchen's clutter preserve might be a specific drawer, a bucket for magazines could be your living room's clutter preserve, and so on. As long as clutter doesn't escape these limited preserves, all is good in the world.

TAKE ACTION NOW: Find one area of your house

that regularly gets messy no how matter how many times you attempt to declutter it and establish a dedicated clutter preserve —be it a chair, drawer, or bucket.

#5

Making It Fun Tip #5: The 300-30 declutter challenge. As its name implies, the 300-30 declutter challenge challenges you to declutter 300 things in 30 days. You can go hardmode and find 300 things to throw out during the next month, or you can simply declutter 300 items by either tossing them, donating, or putting the item back in their proper place.

TAKE ACTION RIGHT NOW: Start your 300-30 declutter challenge today by getting up *right now* and decluttering 10 items. Repeat for the next 29 days.

PART IV: KEEPING YOUR HOME CLUTTER-FREE

#1

Keeping Your Home Clutter-Free Tip #1: Thou shalt obey the one-in one-out rule. In other words, whenever you get something new, you must chuck something else out. If you buy a new pot, pair of shoes, or magazine, an old one must be discarded. The effectiveness of the one-in one-out rule isn't limited to clutter. It can even save you money! Buying a fancy new pasta bowl or coffee mug is no longer so appealing when you know you're going to have to throw out an old favorite. It helps you avoid buying things you don't actually need just because you "feel like it." If you're super-keen to cut the clutter, you can adopt a variation of this rule: The one-in two-out rule. Whenever you get something new, two existing things must go.

TAKE ACTION RIGHT NOW: Not applicable unless you're thinking of purchasing something. If you are, think of one thing you can chuck out or donate.

#2

Keeping Your Home Clutter-Free Tip #2: Create a 30-day list. Want to buy something? Put it on a list and check back in 30 days. (This obviously doesn't apply to essentials such as groceries and fuel.) The idea is that after 30 days that item you wanted so badly no longer seems so appealing. You can look at the purchase more logically rather than getting caught up in the initial emotion and desire. What it comes down to is this: You can declutter all you want, but if you just keep on buying new stuff, it's all going to be for naught. So create a 30-day list and add items that are not absolutely essential.

TAKE ACTION RIGHT NOW: Recently had the urge to buy more stuff that isn't necessary and will do little more than end up as another piece of clutter stuffed next to that ABS-2000 workout machine under the staircase? Then create a 30-day list and put it on it. Trust me, whatever it is you want so badly right now ain't gonna be so appealing in a month's time. And your wallet and cluttered home will be better off because of it.

#3

Keeping Your Home Clutter-Free Tip #3: Use the two F's test. One of the most common pieces of clutter is paper. To combat this, start subjecting any and every new piece of paper entering your home to the two F's test: If you can't file it (e.g. bills and bank statements) or frame it (e.g. kid's artwork), chuck it out.

TAKE ACTION RIGHT NOW: Stop reading this book for a minute or two and go hunt for one piece of paper of the many likely cluttering your home. Now, subject it to the two F's test. If you can't file it or frame it, chuck it in the trash.

#4

Keeping Your Home Clutter-Free Tip #4: Build clutter-busting habits. One of the main reasons people struggle to permanently bust clutter is they have messy habits. They clean out the entire house in one mad dash and then, a week or two later, they find themselves back to square one, as if they'd never decluttered at all. Fortunately, there's a solution (though, word of warning, it's not easy): Build good habits. As I'm sure you know, habits are behaviors that have become automatic and require no thought (such as backing your car out of the driveway). What this means is that if you build clutter-killing habits, clutter won't have a chance to sneak up on you.

TAKE ACTION RIGHT NOW: It takes 66 days (on average) to form a new habit. That's 66 days of consciously executing that clutter-killing action until it because automatic. Here are three potential habits you can start building today: 1) as you get home each evening, shut the door, put the car keys on a hook above the light switch, take off any jackets and coats and hang them on the coat rack, and put your briefcase/purse next to the coats; 2) when bringing in the mail, sort it over the trash can, dump the junk, and file the rest (i.e. anything important) in a plastic sleeve or filing unit on the wall; 3) put things away once you've finished using them—your toothbrush, the TV remote, that cereal box, that empty can of beans, etc.

#5

Keeping Your Home Clutter-Free Tip #5: The two-minute rule. If something takes less than two minutes, do it right away! If you keep procrastinating on these small tasks, they will all gather together and conspire to stress and overwhelm you. They will turn into a tsunami of work that is only more likely to get procrastinated on due to the immensity of its size. So if it's something quick (i.e. two minutes or less), like washing the dirty dishes, chucking some clothes in the washing machine, or putting back a few lost items, do it right away! You could also find some creative uses for the two-minute rule such as by spending two minutes decluttering before or after every meal, or spending two minutes decluttering every time you get home, until—eventually—the clutter is gone!

TAKE ACTION RIGHT NOW: Go find something *right now* that takes two minutes or less. It could be some dirty dishes that need washing, some clothes to go in the washing machine, or some things scattered over the kitchen bench that need to be returned to their proper homes.

PART V: THE KONMARI METHOD

The Kon-What Method?

As you (unfortunately) probably know from personal experience, tidied homes often quickly accumulate clutter again. Fortunately, a cleaning consultant in Japan can help you end this disheartening cluttered-decluttered-cluttered again cycle. Meet Marie Kondo (thus the name of her method, KonMari).

Anyway, here are the basics of her KonMari decluttering method.

#1

KonMari Method Tip #1: Tidy all at once. Marie's advice is to tidy up in one giant push. Though this advice is contrary to the typical "go slow-and-steady so it's not overwhelming" advice, Marie argues that the slow-and-steady approach does not work because there is no jarring, unforgettable transformation. Also, it becomes too easy to lose interest and sink back into your cluttered ways. Marie argues that the jarring transformation inspires you to continue living this way. And that the slow-and-steady approach fails to bring about this permanent change in mindset. Something else she mentions is that it's best to declutter first thing in the morning when your mind is sharp and your focus at its peak.

TAKE ACTION RIGHT NOW: Schedule a weekend when you're free and can make that "one giant push" toward completely decluttering your home.

#2

KonMari Method Tip #2: Visualize. If you find yourself struggling to get started (or complete) a big decluttering session, visualize what your home will look like when it's free of clutter. You can also use this visualization technique *before* decluttering to help you identify what should be thrown out and what should be kept. Visualize your ideal, clutter-free home to help you make decisions and to inspire you to declutter.

TAKE ACTION RIGHT NOW: Don't worry, this is an easy one. So actually do it. *Right now.* Here it is: Visualize what you home will look like once it is completely decluttered.

#3

KonMari Method Tip #3: **Thou shalt tidy by category, not room.** This aspect of the KonMari method also runs contrary to conventional decluttering advice. The reason for this is that most people have similar items stored all around the house, not just in one room. The problem with tidying one room at a time, Marie argues, is that you'll likely fail to realize just how much of something you have. By tidying by category, you avoid this problem.

TAKE ACTION RIGHT NOW: Marie suggests the following order: Clothes, books, papers, and then miscellaneous items. (Remember to separate these categories into subcategories, such as pants, tops, socks, coats, etc.) So get started using the KonMari method right now by decluttering your closet!

#4

KonMari Method Tip #4: Determine if an item "sparks joy". The idea behind this tip is to not focus solely on chucking everything out in your effort to declutter, but to declutter everything that does not bring you joy. You want to have a few things that you cherish rather than a house full of clutter that stresses you out. You do *not* want a house devoid of everything, as that too will bring unhappiness. Marie advises you hold each item in your hands and ask yourself whether or not the item "sparks joy." The idea behind actually holding the item is that this is an intuitive process. You *feel* it.

TAKE ACTION RIGHT NOW: Go find a piece of clutter in your home, hold it in your hands, and ask yourself: "Does this spark joy?" If it's a non-essential item (e.g. not a bed or knife) and it doesn't spark joy, then toss it. Keep the things that spark joy and get rid of the rest. You'll be all the happier for it.

Conclusion

Decluttering your home will leave you feeling lighter, happier, and freer.

The tips in this book *will* work and they'll help you beat that gnawing sense of stress and overwhelm that a cluttered home instills in you. Even though these tips work, you need to take action. If you haven't taken action as prescribed by the "Take Action Right Now" sections below each tip, then go back, review them, and do as they say.

If you don't take action, nothing will change.

If you *do* act on the 37 ways to declutter your home taught in this book, then a clutter-free home is yours for the taking.

Good luck.

(Actually, scratch that. You don't need luck, because I know you're going to take action and declutter your home. Action beats luck every time. So... *Happy decluttering!*)

Made in the USA
Middletown, DE
24 May 2017